THAT BIG BAD WOLF

Published by Bernadette Gilligan

First published 2013, Palmer Higgs Pty Ltd

Second Edition 2017

© 2017 Bernadette Gilligan

The moral right of the author has been asserted.

All rights reserved. Without limiting the rights under copyright restricted above, no part of this publication may be reproduced, stored in or introduced into a retrieval system, or transmitted, in any form or by any means (electronic, mechanical, photocopying, recording or otherwise), without the prior written permission of both the copyright owner and the above publisher of this book.

This book is a work of fiction. All characters in this book are fictitious and any resemblance to actual persons, living or dead, is purely coincidental.

A Cataloguing–in–Publication record is available from the National Library of Australia.

ISBN: 978-0-6480988-0-5 (pbk)

Illustrator: Liz Imbriano

THAT BIG BAD WOLF

BERNADETTE GILLIGAN

Especially for My children,
Jai, Dean, Aaron, Nick and Jenae.

My grandchildren,
Chloe-Jade, Izabella, Cayden, Tayah, Mason
and the many more to come.

Lotza luv Nana G ☺

A special thanks to Uncle Wal.

A note from Nana G,

My inspiration for writing this book began around 1994 when I was working at the Beenleigh Police Citizens Youth Club, Qld. I was child minding for all the mums that wanted a break and went to play bingo.

I started reading the old fables to the young children and found that quite a few of them were scared by the endings of these stories. So I began reading the books with a less frightening ending.

For some unknown reason the tune of the five little ducks came into my head and I started a rhyming song in my head. I grabbed some paper and put it all together.

The words in this book were used for a play that I put on for the Burrows Primary School, Marsden, Qld. around 1996. I had been very involved in the Beenleigh theatre group and took direction from what I had learned there. I auditioned the children in grade 2 and taught the class to sing the words to the tune of the 5 little ducks. We did this as a fundraiser.

I hope your children enjoy my story, and remember you can always have a sing along with them as well.

Lotza luv Nana G ☺

Three little pigs left home one day,
Over the hills and far away,
Mother pig said "go make your own homes
It's time for you all to be alone",

The first little pig made a house of straw,
He wasn't rich, he was quite poor,

The second little pig made a house of sticks,
He couldn't be bothered with water and mix,

The third little pig made a house of bricks,
He was the one with all the tricks,

The other pigs left their homes,
With lots and lots of moans and groans,
Because the big bad wolf blew their homes away,

They both ran to their brothers home that day,

The pig that was in the house of brick,
Was getting ready for the biggest trick,

Down the chimney came the wolf that was bold,
Straight into a pot that was icy cold,

He ran away doing a kind of jig,
Never to be seen again by the pigs.

www.ingramcontent.com/pod-product-compliance
Lightning Source LLC
Chambersburg PA
CBHW042052290426
44110CB00001B/40